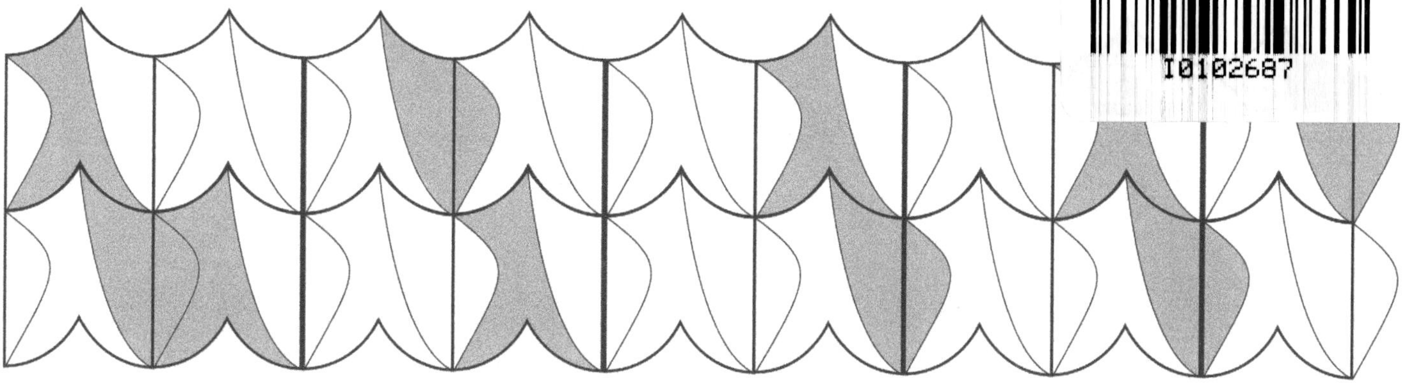

Sophisticate's Coloring Book

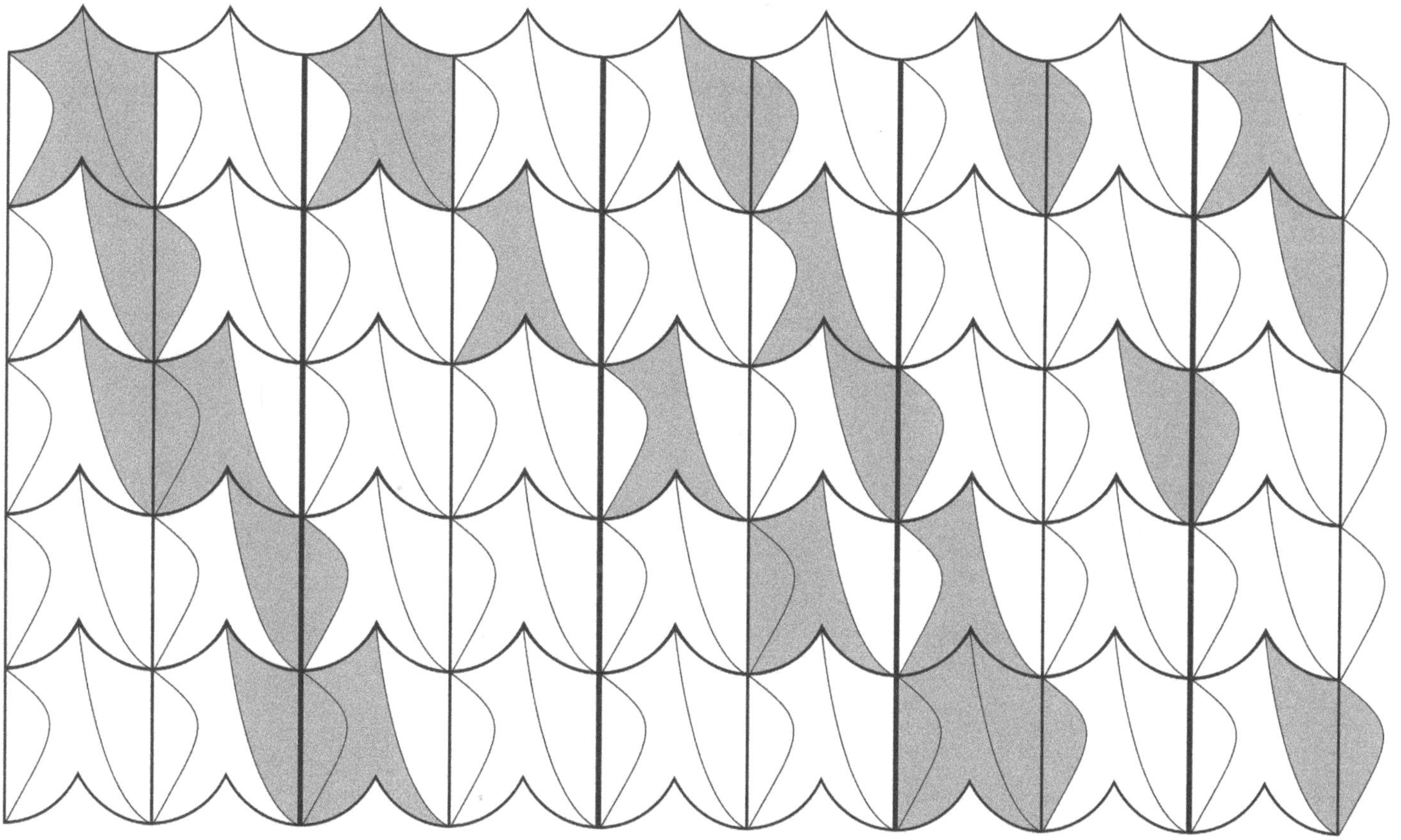

Copyright © 2016 by Jimmy Hines. All rights reserved. Not for reproduction.
ISBN-10: 0692644148 ISBN-13: 978-0692644140

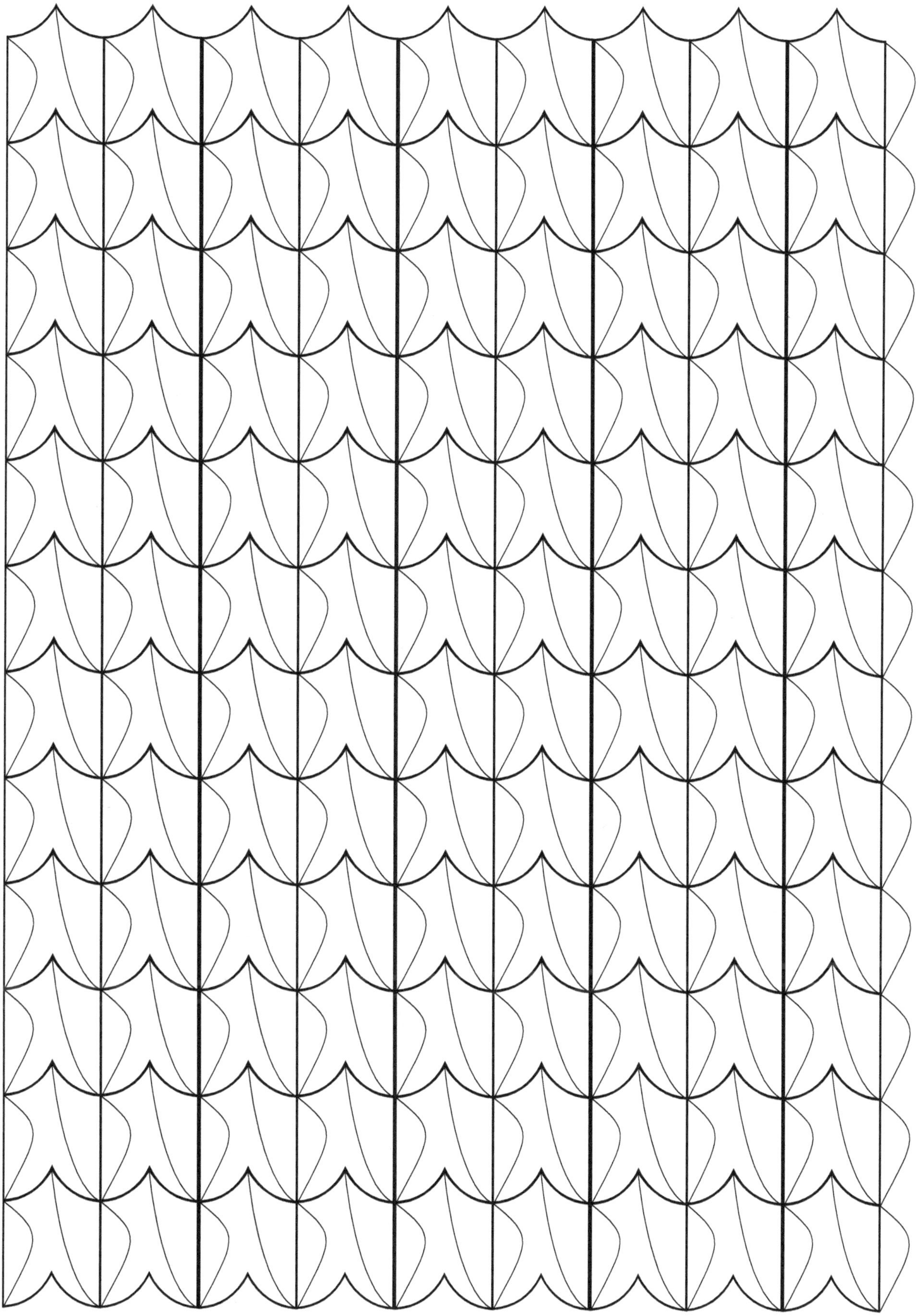

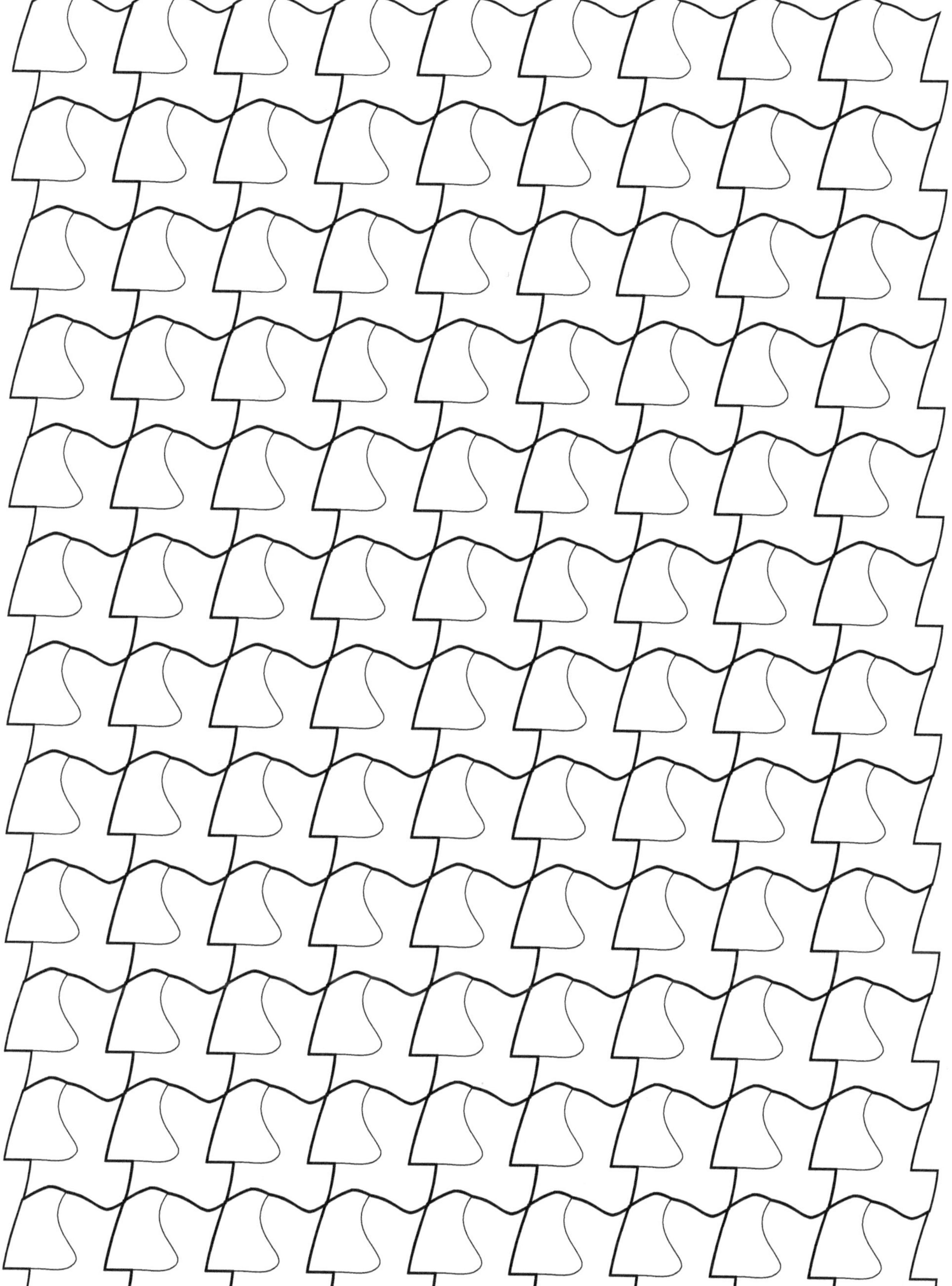

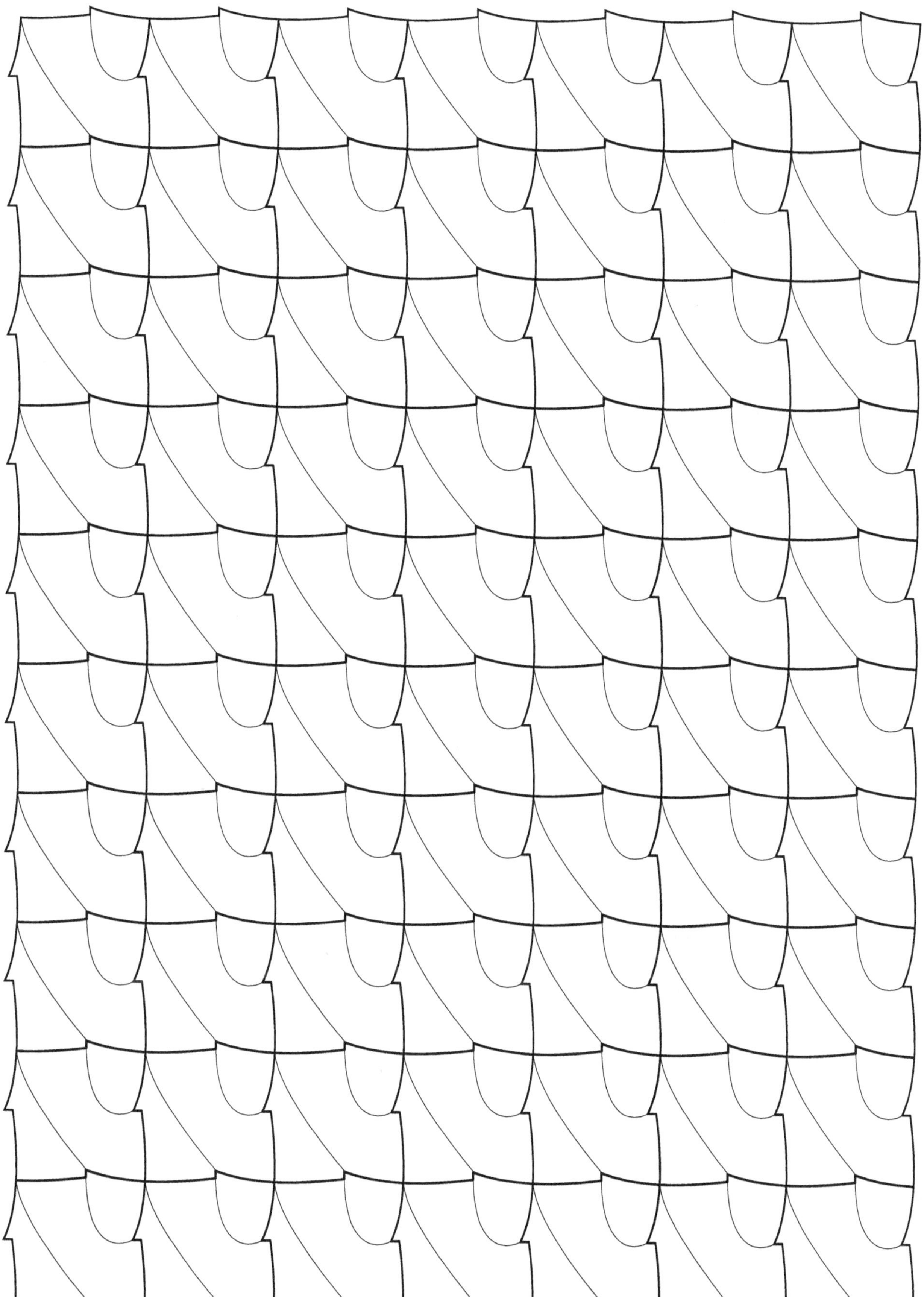

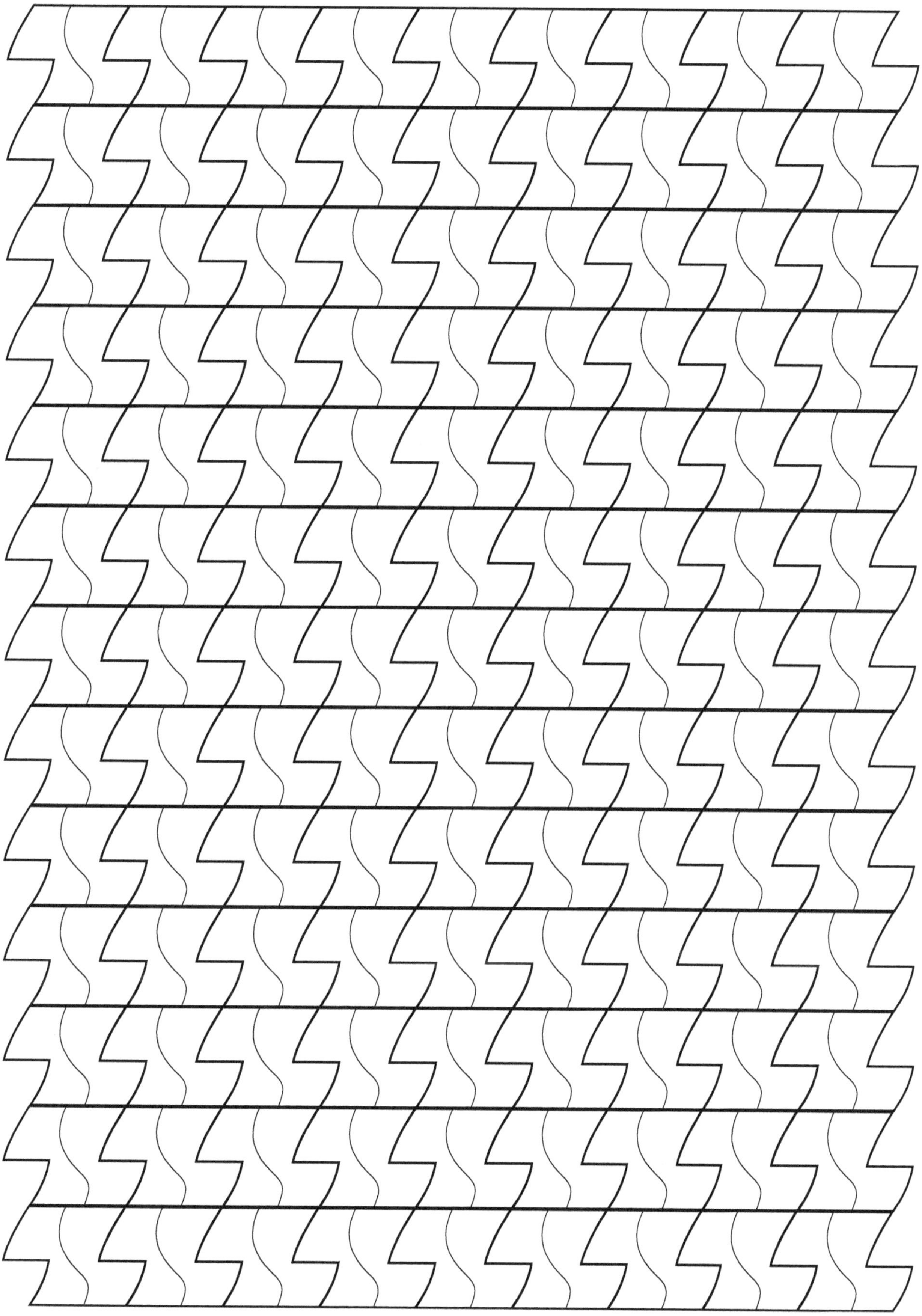

www.ingramcontent.com/pod-product-compliance
Lightning Source LLC
Chambersburg PA
CBHW081652270326
41933CB00018B/3445